Thomas Worlidge, Dryden Leach, James Wicksteed

A Select Collection of Drawings from Curious Antique Gems

Vol. 2

Thomas Worlidge, Dryden Leach, James Wicksteed

A Select Collection of Drawings from Curious Antique Gems
Vol. 2

ISBN/EAN: 9783337320133

Printed in Europe, USA, Canada, Australia, Japan

Cover: Foto ©Thomas Meinert / pixelio.de

More available books at **www.hansebooks.com**

A

SELECT COLLECTION

OF

DRAWINGS

FROM

CURIOUS ANTIQUE GEMS.

A

SELECT COLLECTION

OF

DRAWINGS

FROM

CURIOUS ANTIQUE GEMS;

MOST OF THEM IN THE POSSESSION OF THE NOBILITY
AND GENTRY OF THIS KINGDOM.

ETCHED AFTER THE MANNER OF REMBRANDT,

BY T. WORLIDGE, PAINTER.

VOL II.

LONDON:

PRINTED BY DRYDEN LEACH,

FOR M. WORLIDGE, GREAT QUEEN-STREET, LINCOLN's-INN-
FIELDS; AND M. WICKSTEED, SEAL-ENGRAVER AT BATH.
MDCCLXVIII.

Sapho *on Paste L.d Montague*.

according to act of Parliament *J. Mortidge S.*

Mercury on Red Agate. L.d Montagu
according to Act of Parliament   S. Worlidge &

Cicero on *Beryl* . Mr *Hope* .

According to Act of Parliament   *W. Richardson sc.*

Infant Hercules *on Intaglio. Mat. Duane Esq.*

According to Act of Parliament. *T. Worlidge sc.*

Minerva on Crisolite Ld. Montague.

A Mask of Silenus. *on Cor. Duke of Marlborough.*

drawing to the of Parliament. *C. Worlidge sculp.*

A Lyon on Beryl Hon.ble Mr Robinson.

according to dei of Parbament.

C Winbels f. 18

Julia on Cornelian Lord Montague.
according to act of Parliament   J Wedulge sc.

Neptune *on* Jar: L.^d. Montague
according to Act of Parliament   T. Worlidge sculp.

Meſsalina *Yellow Cor. Ld. Montague*

drawn by &c. Pohaton   *J. Hobday sculp*

Philosopher, Onex, Dutch: of Portland.

According to the Act of Parliament   *T. Worlidge sc.*

Medusa on Cor. Tho.ᵉ Dundaſ. Esq.ʳ
according to the Act of Parliament T. Worlidge &c.

Cupid & Boar, on Am. Tho.ͤ Dundaſ's Eſq.ͬ

according to Act of Parliament.   J. Rutledge &c.

Hercules on Cor. Tho.ᵈ Dundas's Esqʳ.

According to Act of Parliament.   T. Birbige sc.

A Sow on Cor.^l Thos Dundass Esqr
according to Act of Parliament at Westm.^r &c.

Dea della Salute *en Ame. Mr Hope*

According to Act of Parliament   *& Worlidge sc*

Apollo, on Cornelian. Duke of Marlborough.

according to act of Parliament   T. Worlidge sculp.

Caius Marius *on* Cor *D^r* *Chauncey*.

Medusa *on Topaz* M.ʳ Hope

according to Act of Parliament   *T. Worledge sculp.*

Cleopatra an Intaglio In.º Tomlinson Esq.ʳ
according to Act of Parliament   G. Woodfoe sc.

Hercules bibax on Cor. Duke of Marlborough?
according to Act of Parliament   T. Worlidge sc.

Silenus on Onyx L.ᵈ Clanbrassill

According to Act of Parliament   T. Worlidge &c.

Diomede *on White Agate.* P. Snell *Jun.*

According to Act of Parliament J. Worlidge St.

An Urn on Red Jasper; the Hon.ble M.r Robinson.

According to Act of Parliament. L. Morlidge St.

ΟΥΟΛΟΥ

Jupiter Serips on Beryl. D'. Chauncey.

according to the L' Parliament   & Worlidge sc

Horse &c. on Corn: Duke of Marlborough.

According to Act of Parliament.   *T. Worlidge Sc.*

Lepidus *on Beryl L*ᵈ *Beſsbrough.*

according to Act of Parliament   J. Worlidge c.

A Bachanal *on Cor. Mr. Stanley.*
According to Act of Parliam.t   *J. Woolidge sc.*

Agrippina *on Beryl* Ld *Bessborough*

Philip of Macedon *on Beryl L^d. Befsboro*.

according to Act of Parliament T Worlidge sc.

Mercury on Beryl Duke of. Marlborough .?.

according to Act of Parliament .

Alexander *on Cor. L.d Bessborough?*

According to Act of Parliament. *F. Woolidge &c.*

Tiberius *on Cor.* L.d Bessborough *.*

According to Act of Parliament.   T. Worlidge *sc.*

Marcus Brutus *en Ber. L.ᵈ Bessborough* .

According to Act of Parliament. *S. Woodidge Sc.*

Ptolomy on Topaz. L.ᵈ Bessborough.
According to Act of Parliament.   T. Milidge S.

Jupiter Ammon *en Cor.Ld Bessborough.*

According to Act of Parliament. *T. Woolidge Sc.*

A Vacca, on Onix D.ᵣ Chauncey.

According to Act of Parliament.   T. Wedilds &c.

Ptolemy *en Ber.* *D.ʳ Chauncy.*

According to Act of Parliament. *J. Wooledge. Sc.*

Lucilla *on* *Beryl* *L:* *Befsborough.*

according to Act of Parliament   *T. Worlidge &c.*

Caraculla, *on Saph.* D.ⁿ Bessborough.

Recording to Act of Parliament. T. Worlidge, fe.

Jole, on Am. L.ᵈ Beſsborough.
According to Act of Parliament T. Wedgwood. &c.

Pluto, on Cor. L.ᵈ Beſsborough?
(According to Act of parliament. J. Woolidge. ſc.

Hannibal *on Agate L.ᵈ Bessborough.*
According to Act of Parliament. *T. Worlidge Sc.*

Metrodorus *en Cor. P.ᵗ Bessborough*
According to Act of Parliament. *C.F. Wolledge, s.c.*

Sapho *en Cor. Ld Besaberough l.*
According to Act of Parliament. *T. Worlidge s fe.*

Bacchus, on Aqua Marina Duke of Marlborough
Accordant to Act of Parliament

Jupiter Seraphi, en Am. L. Bessborough.
according to Act of Parliament. *Seal's delg. e*

A Faun *en Cer.* *L.* *Bessborough.*

Drawing : R.^t Dalcmaine. *T. Radcliffe. S.*

Julia Pia, en Aqua Marin. L.ᵈ Besborough.
According to Act of Parliament.   T. Worlidge &c

Scipio Africanus, *on Cor. Strozzi, Rome.*
According to Act of parliament. *J. Woolidge, sc.*

A Philosopher, on Corn. M.ͬ Stanley.

According to Act of Parliam.ͭ . T. Worlidge Sc.

Sabina, *on Rev.* Duke *of* Marlborough.

According to Act of Parliament. T. Woolidge *sc.*

A Satyr, on Cor. Florentine. 2.

According to Act of Parliament.   Sh. Woolidge sc.

Homer, *on Ber. L.ᵈ Radnor.*
According to Act of Parliament by J. Woolidge etc.

Baccant on Beryl L.ᵈ Befsborough

According to Act of Parliament   G. Worlidge &c

Hercules, *on an Onyx, Duke of Portland.*
Qu. dion? Act of Parliam.   *C. Reveley del.*

Epicurus, on Onyx, D.ʳ Chauncey.
According to Ant. of Herculan. *T. Woolidge.*

Vitellius, enCor: Mr Stanley.

Accordning to Act of Parliam: T.Woolidge sc.

A Mask, on Beryl. M.ᵉ Stanley.

According to Act of Parliament d. Worlidge &

Diomede & Ulysses on *Sarde* Duke of Marlborough

Accoraing to Act of Parliament. J. Worlidge Sculp

A Faun *on Ber. Lord Warwick.*

according to Act of Parl:ament   *C. Kirkidge sc.*

Chimera on Sar. M.ᵗ Stanley.

Pursuant to Act of Parliament   T Worlidge sc.

Jupiter Ammon. *en Ber*
Duke of Leeds.

According to Act of Parliament *A. Burtledge Sculp.*

www.ingramcontent.com/pod-product-compliance
Lightning Source LLC
Chambersburg PA
CBHW032009010726
47493CB00007B/2330